SMALL BUSINESS FITNESS

SMALL BUSINESS FITNESS

Simple Exercises for Entrepreneurial Health

Stuart Preston

iUniverse, Inc.
New York Lincoln Shanghai

Small Business Fitness
Simple Exercises for Entrepreneurial Health

iUniverse books may be ordered through booksellers or by contacting:

iUniverse
2021 Pine Lake Road, Suite 100
Lincoln, NE 68512
www.iuniverse.com
1-800-Authors (1-800-288-4677)

ISBN-13: 978-0-595-38027-5 (pbk)
ISBN-13: 978-0-595-82397-0 (ebk)
ISBN-10: 0-595-38027-1 (pbk)
ISBN-10: 0-595-82397-1 (ebk)

Printed in the United States of America

Special Thanks to Suzanne Babb and my wife Cynthia for all their help in getting this thing readable. Also Thanks to my family for putting up with night after night of me and my laptop.

Additional thanks go to all of my business school teachers, partners, customers, clients, associates, employees, bosses, and others who taught me the lessons in these pages. Thank you all.

Contents

Introduction

I've been told that my skill as a business consultant is being able to take a large, complicated subject and make it simple and understandable. Well, that is what I'm doing here. You own your business. If I had to guess, I'd say you have very little time for strategizing, for looking at the big picture, for seeing things from 10,000 feet. I know because I've been there. It's nearly impossible for an entrepreneur to have the General's perspective of the battle when he/she has to be down in the trenches.

Over the last fifteen years, I've experienced entrepreneurship, military leadership, academia, and independent sales. I've gathered a lot of knowledge about what works and what doesn't work when it comes to running a successful small business. What every business owner needs is a system around which he/she can maintain a view from above, to see which direction his/her business is going, in order to make the necessary adjustments. It is these adjustments and decisions that will determine if the business survives and, if it does survive, how successful it will be.

As you read through this book, I bet a few brainstorms will fire off and you will come up with some original, great ideas for your company. If that happens, do two things. Put into your calendar time to analyze the idea and develop a plan of action for it. Then, make a note in the back of this workbook so that you will always have that idea at hand.

The key is to act NOW on that idea. I have a principle I call the Preston Principle of Procrastination. Basically, it states that once you have an idea, the probability (likelihood) of you taking action on that idea diminishes proportional to the time that passes since you had the idea. If you have the idea today and you wait until tomorrow to act, chances are 50% that you will in fact take action. The next day your chances are 33%. For you math types, the formula is (where P is Probability, T is Time since Idea):

$$P_{Action}(Idea)_{T \to \infty} = \frac{1}{T}$$

Okay, enough of that.

I hope you get two things from this workbook. First, I hope it inspires you. Second, I hope it gives you the tools you need to guide your small business to success.

Enjoy,

Stuart

CHAPTER 1

▼

DEVELOPING AN "IN THE ZONE" FOCUS

Most success books, from the <u>Seven Habits</u> to <u>Rich Dad</u> to <u>Good to Great</u>, will have a similar theme: spend your time doing what contributes to your goals and spend NO time on those tasks that don't. What this means to you is Focus. A Focus on your goals and your purpose in life is a must. Such a focus will help you make good decisions and make those decisions easier. For example, when you started your first business and that envelope came with a promotional pen inside, you had to make a decision: to buy or not to buy the pen. It was not just any pen, mind you, but a pen with your company name on it. Bet you wanted that pen. I did. I had a box of 500 of them in my office closet for years. Bad decision. If I had been focused, deciding NOT to buy those pens would have been an easy decision, and I would have had some extra bread in my marketing basket. Will the pens contribute to your business? A strong focus will help you decide.

So how do we develop a proper Focus on the business? Easy. First, you must rediscover the passion you had for your business when you first started. Second, become familiar with your vision of success—I call it the Moment of Success. A picture of that moment is in your head right now. Third, develop a method for keeping a focus on that vision. In business terms, this is having a Mission Statement, a Vision Statement, a list of Values, and knowing your Sustainable Competitive Advantage. That last one will make sense later. Fourth, we will identify the proper business strategy for your company. This strategy is the plan to get your company to the Vision. Easy. Finally, we will fill out a Dashboard which clearly identifies and states your company's goals and objectives.

So, five simple steps, when put into real practice, will get you the focus you need to make good decisions and make them with little effort. This is your compass which points directly to long-term success. Now let's get to work.

Passion

Think back to the moment you decided to go into business for the first time. You were filled with excitement, optimism, and hope. In other words, you were passionate about your plans. You had large ideas and no doubts about making them a reality. You filled out all the red-tape (it was probably the only time you've been happy to fill out government paperwork!). It is this passion that you need to reconnect with.

Another moment to recall is the moment you realized (or believed) there is a market for your skills/products: "I KNOW people will want this!" Whether or not you were right, you had a rush of excitement we're calling Passion. Try to relive whichever moment it was that you felt passionate about your new venture.

It is essential to your success that you are able to feel this passion for your business. In other parts of your life, you reconnect with the original passion that helps you sustain your efforts, from the care of your vehicle to your marriage. With your business, it is just as essential that you are able to bring out that passion and feed off of its energy.

Moment of Success

You have a vision of the Moment of Success in your mind right now. Close your eyes and think about the words, "I've made it!" What do you see? Take a mental picture of this Moment of Success. This is the personal side of maintaining a focus on your business' success. You have a personal stake in your company's success, and this vision is what will help you get to that moment. Keep this image in your mind and focus your efforts toward getting there. When you come to making a decision, the answer should be one that helps you reach your Moment of Success.

The Mission Statement

The Mission Statement is a description of your company's reason for being. Why does your company exist? The mission statement is one of the most important concepts you will develop in this workbook. The rest of the issues here will be centered around this statement. Make sure you take time to create a meaningful and effective mission statement.

Your mission statement must meet the following criteria:

1. Clearly states your reason for being

2. Communicates your image/identity

3. Provides direction for the future

4. Short (2 sentences max)

5. Inspirational, instills pride and enthusiasm

6. Clear, concise, focused—to the benefits, not the products

7. Measurable, but not quantifiable (not a specific goal)

8. May include company values

Here are some examples of good mission statements:

- "Our mission is to inform, inspire, and empower people and organizations to be their best—both personally and professionally."—Success Networks

- "We will market the most appealing and widely worn casual clothing in the world. We will clothe the world."—Levi Strauss

- "The mission of Southwest Airlines is dedication to the highest quality of Customer Service delivered with a sense of warmth, friendliness, individual pride, and Company Spirit."—Southwest Airlines

- "Google's mission is to organize the world's information and make it universally accessible and useful."—Google

The Vision Statement

Take a look at your mission statement. If you lead your company into the future using your mission statement, where will it take you? Where will it take you in your market, in sales, in innovation? A single, inspiration, grand statement of where your company will be in five-to-ten years will be a good vision statement.

Company Values

In this day and age of business scandals and lapses in ethics, it is very important for you to maintain your company's values. These values must be displayed for your employees and for your customers. Most importantly, they must be inherent in everything you do. A great example is a sign displayed at a petroleum/lubricants facility: "No job is too important and no service too urgent for us to get it done in anything but a SAFE manner!" They value safety and everybody knows it.

Sustainable Competitive Advantage

I have tried to stay away from esoteric business terms (like 'esoteric') in this workbook, but I can't avoid Sustainable Competitive Advantage. In essence, this is an edge you hold over your competition which they cannot overcome—sustainable.

Now, what advantage do you have that your competition cannot match? Easy, its YOU. You have a history, a character, a story that cannot be told or replicated by your competition. In this story is you ability to create a unique experience for your customer, and experience that no other company can reproduce. You need to figure out how your story (your history) has led you to a place where you can offer a unique product or service to your customer.

A great example of this concept is in a Harvard Case Study about a man named Bernard Horowitz. Bernard worked in his parents' New York deli starting at age thirteen. He grew up on a true, authentic New York Jewish deli. As an adult, he spent a few years in the Air Force, ending up in Hawaii. He stayed there and opened up a New York deli. It was a raging success. Competition tried to match his success, but they could not. Bernard had the history from which he translated a unique experience for his customers: the smells, the menu, the food, the attitude of a true New York Jewish deli. That…is a sustainable competitive advantage, and you have it, too!

Strategy

Identifying your business' strategy is as simple as understanding the basic types of strategy. First, we have a Market Strategy, which is the overall focus of our marketing efforts. Then, we have the Business Strategy, which is how you execute the operations of your business.

The Market Strategies are:

1. Low-Cost: Your focus is on the consumer who is price-focused and you do everything you can to reduce expenses, e.g. WalMart.

2. Differentiation: You aim for the general masses, but do it in a slightly different way, e.g. Target.

3. Focus/Niche: You aim away from the masses and towards a small segment of the market, e.g. Nieman Marcus.

4. Speed: You do it faster than anybody else, e.g. FedEx

The Business Strategies are:

1. Concentration: You focus on your craft so that you do it better than anybody else, keeping a separation in the market, e.g. Rolex.

2. Innovation: You focus on being cutting-edge in advancement, e.g. Apple.

3. Market Development: Take an existing product and expand it into new markets, e.g. Baking Soda

4. Product Development: Develop new products for existing markets, e.g. Gillette

The Exercises: An "In the Zone" Focus

Passion

If, when you wake up tomorrow, your business was all about one single product or service, which would it be? Which product or service of yours really gets you pumped up about your business? Describe the product and WHAT, specifically, you enjoy about it:

_____

_____

_____

_____

Again, if that was the only product you had, finish the sentence: What I'm really passionate about is

_____

_____

Think back to the time you were just getting started. You were filling out the government paperwork. You were designing logos and business cards. You were letting everybody know about your business. You were filled with excitement and passion. Describe that time here:

_____

_____

_____

_____

Vision

Take a mental picture of your Moment of Success. Close your eyes and picture the moment well into the future when your BUSINESS has been a success for a few years. What does it look like? A store on every corner? Awards? An office in Hong Kong? What else? Take a mental Polaroid of that moment and describe it here:

_____

_____

_____

_____

Now, summarize that image into a single sentence. Make it a grand statement of large success:

_____

_____

_____

This is your Vision Statement.

Mission Statement

1. Plan a full day to dedicate to developing your Mission Statement

2. Get everybody involved

3. Issue general guidelines for the statement:

   a. Concise: Two sentences max

    b. Inspirational

    c. Focused on benefits, not products

    d. Communicates your Reason for Being

    e. Communicates your image and identity

    f. Measurable, but not quantifiable (not a specific goal)

    g. Contains company values

4. Present ideas with open minds

5. Select best options

6. Fine tune and select the single best option

Write your Mission Statement here:

_____

_____

_____

Get your Mission Statement posted in your office where all can see.

Include reading your Mission Statement in your weekly meetings.

Quiz your employees to see if they can repeat the Mission Statement.

Values

Write a list of your company's values, such as:

Integrity

Innovation

Ethics

Creativity

Honesty

Leadership

Customer Service

Good humor

Speed

Innovation

Freedom

Excellence

Respect

- _____

- _____

- _____

- _____

- _____

Sustainable Competitive Advantage

Write a short biography (1–3 paragraphs), paying specific attention to the experiences in life that helped you become the ONLY person in your market that can provide the unique experience that your company offers. Think about past work history, relationships that taught you the business, school, etc. Write it here:

_____

_____

_____

_____

_____

_____

_____

_____

_____

_____

_____

_____

_____

_____

_____

Read the above biography, or have somebody else read it. How do your experiences translate into a unique experience for your customer? Think about your product design, development and delivery. What about those processes are different from your competition because of your experiences? Describe your Sustainable Competitive Advantage here:

_____

_____

_____

Strategy

Select a Market Strategy

- Low-Cost

- Differentiation

- Speed

- Focus/Niche

Select a Business Strategy

- Concentration

- Innovation

- Market Development

- Product Development

CHAPTER 2

▼

MARKETING

The key to marketing your products is knowing why your company exists. What do I mean by that? How does your product fill a need in your target market? What is it about your products, goods and services that bring customers to your door? This is your company's Raison D'être, its "reason for being." The reason your company exists is to serve this market.

The goal of your marketing program is to make Sales easier. Peter Drucker put it best: "The ultimate aim of marketing is to make sales superfluous." In other words, your marketing efforts should result in your market coming to you for your products. So, we need to figure out *why* your market comes to you. Do you do it faster than anybody else? Is your product different? How are you meeting their needs?

Your marketing efforts should be proactive to your market, rather than reactive. By getting to know your market intimately, you will be able to respond to changes in the market. You will continue to build products that satisfy their needs and desires, thereby ensuring your place within the market.

There are four key areas to marketing, known as the Four P's of Marketing:

1. Product

2. Price

3. Place

4. Promotion

Product

The most obvious part of your marketing plan is your product, whether that is a product line, a single product, a good, or a service. Whichever of these is appropriate to your business, we will call it your 'product.' In developing your products, it becomes too easy to become infatuated with the product itself or the process of making it. What is more important to your success is how this product meets the needs of your market. So, how do you design your products to match your markets demands?

You can find what your market thirsts for by asking them. First, ask your customers. Ask them how they feel about your past dealings. Ask them what they like and dislike about both your products and your service. Go through your invoices and receipts to find which products sell the best, which ones are returned the most, which ones have the most repeat sales.

Next, ask your entire market what they think. How? Do a market survey. You will have to define your target market. If you've been in business for a few years, this will be almost intuitively easy. If you're new, it will take a little thinking. What I recommend my clients do is draw up a biography of a 'person' who represents your market. Give that person a name, like Chris or Jodi or Jane or John, whatever. Describe what he or she wants out of life. How old is she/he? How much income does he/she have? Where does she/he live? Define this market representative down to the last detail. This is your target market. In the exercises section, there are example questions and some recommended questions to ask on your survey. A good place to launch a survey is www.zoomerang.com. They have all kinds of resources for getting your survey designed and launched.

Additionally, let's get the creative juices flowing by dreaming up a magic product that, if you had it would clean up your market and send your competition running. I call this THE ONE THING. What is the one thing that would pave your path to market domination? For example, if Microsoft or Dell could make a computer that turns on like a light bulb, that would be THE ONE THING that would slaughter their competition. What is THE ONE THING in your market? The key here is to let your brain free to think outside the box. The point of this exercise is to get you to think like your target customer. What one feature, benefit, function, or product would change their lives and make them buy your product over every other competitor's product?

Finally, let's take a look at how your product is meeting your customers' needs. To do this, we'll go back a little to psychologist Abraham Maslow, who proposed, in his 1943 paper *A Theory of Human Motivation,* a hierarchy of human needs. They are as follows:

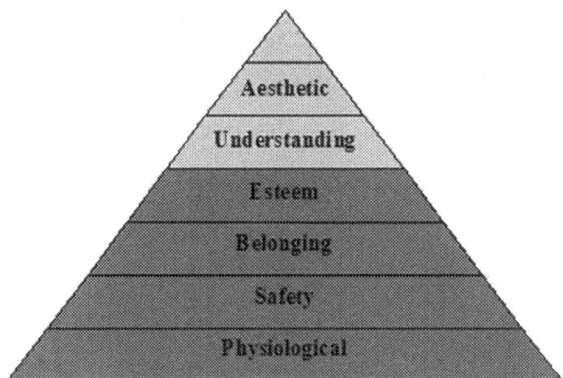

Your products likely fill one or more of the above needs. The needs are defined as:

1. Physiological: comfort, activity, exercise, food, water, air

2. Safety: security

3. Belonging: love, acceptance, clubs, work groups, religious groups, family, gangs

4. Esteem: respect, recognition

5. Understanding: knowledge, education, learning

6. Aesthetic: symmetry, order, beauty

Think about your products. When your customers buy your product, what basic need are they looking to satisfy? Now, this is getting a little over the top in business theory, I admit. However, the point to take from this is that your products are helping your customers satisfy some need, urge, itch, desire, etc. It's important to understand this as you develop and market these products.   I t will be a big help in the sales efforts if you can easily communicate to your customer how your product is going to make his/her life better.

Price

The next 'P' of marketing is Price. The primary concept to know about Price is that it is set by your market, NOT by your financial statements. Price is a simple function of supply and demand. The price is in the minds and hearts of your customers. It is the value they perceive your product to have. My Dad always said a purchase is "only expensive if you paid too much for it!" Good advice. It's about the perceived value of a thing.

So how do you find the right price? Well, you can test the market. Put a price tag on it and see if it sells. If it does, try slowly raising the price. If it doesn't, first analyze your promotion efforts, then try adjusting down a little bit. Alternately, you can be clever and go find out what your competition is charging. If you have similar products, check them out, then adjust your product up or down based on the different features your product offers.

If you are lucky enough to reach full capacity in your sales and fulfillment abilities, you have two options. First, you can raise your prices a little bit, as demand has now swelled past supply. Second, you can start cherry-picking your customers. Only do business with the best of the best customers. Speaking of this, I always recommend service businesses weed out the bottom 10–15% percent of its client base each year or two. These are the clients who are paying old rates or who are difficult to satisfy. Start rotating your client stock.

Place

I have two definitions for 'Place.' First is distribution. How are you placing your products in front of your customers? Is it on a shelf in a store? On the internet? In a catalog? Sometimes the placement of a product is the key factor in determining that product's success. Are you selling wholesale or retail? Do you need to be one or the other, not both? As an example of placement, let's consider a favorite American pastime: beer. There are two basic types of beers: the craft beer and the football beer (you know, the Buds, Millers, Coors, etc.). Now, when you go to buy a six-pack of beer, these two types of beer are on opposite ends of the beer aisle. So, when you go to buy your favorite brew, you head directly to one end of the aisle or the other. If I was to market beer, I'd have to know: do I place my beer in the craft section or the football beer section. The same consideration must be made when you decide to place your product in front of your market. Where are they? Where will they look for your product?

The second part of this marketing 'P' is Position. This is really key to your marketing efforts. Positioning is much like Place. In the example above, if I was to make a new craft beer, I'd have to find a hole in the craft beer market and position my beer in that hole. For example, if I spend time making the best pale ale out there, I'd have to position it as such in this beer aisle. I might want to sell it in larger singles and give it a really high price (how's a $20 bottle of beer sound?). What I don't want to do is try to undercut the price of my competitors and/or place this quality beer in the football beer section. Its *position* in the market must send the right message to the customer.

How are your products positioned? High price and high quality? Great value?

Take a look at the following chart. Each bubble is a company within a market. The size of the bubble indicates the size of the company. The bubble's position indicates its Cost-to-Quality ratio. In the automobile market, the Kias and Hyundais would be on the bottom left, the GMs and Fords in the middle, and the BMWs and Mercedes in the top right. Where are you and your competitors in this type of scenario?

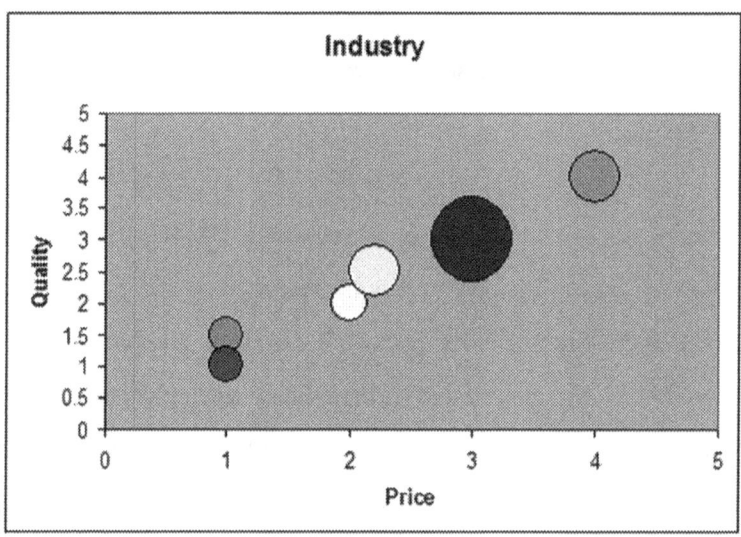

Promotion

Now that you know you have a great product, you've priced it to sell, and you've placed it in front of your customer, you have to tell your market all about it. This is called Promotion. In a nutshell, there are a few general methods of promotion, and you should integrate them all (or most of them) into a good promotional mix that surrounds your market. Look at your promotional effort in military terms. You are going to surround your market and not let them out without them first seeing your promos eleven times. That's right, eleven times! According to Susan Kricun of Kricun Inc. it takes eleven touches to get your customers to act and make a purchase.

The easiest form of Promotion is advertising. This is also probably the most erratic, hit-and-miss method out there. Most small businesses go for advertising in order to avoid doing cold calling or direct sales. Advertising should be looked at as a way of making one of those eleven touches, not a sole method for promoting your products.

The close cousin of advertising is public relations. This is getting the word out there for free by getting the new outlets to treat it like a story. There is a book out there called the Finder Binder that will list all of the media contacts in your area. Be sure to buy one of these and let them know when you have news-worthy events. This could be new products, recently completed projects, industry news, whatever might be interesting to the news folks. Target your press releases to magazines, newspapers, television and radio. The key here is to properly integrate it with your advertising efforts to maintain your message and identity.

Direct marketing, in the form of mailings, is the next most-often used source by entrepreneurs. It seems easy to launch 5000 postcards and expect some business. You need to read your new marketing plan to make sure you are filling the right mailboxes with your postcards and that the postcards have the right message. If you miss on either one, you are likely to face real disappointment.

Finally, and everybody's favorite, is direct sales. Making those cold calls or knocking on doors is not fun for anybody, but it does have good returns and is a good way to get the message out to your customers. See the Sales chapter for a good cold calling format.

Again, it is important that your marketing plan includes a MIX of these forms of promotions. Hit your target market from multiple angles, multiple times, and you will turn them into customers!

The Exercises: Marketing

Customer Survey

Conduct a Customer Survey on your clients. The goal of the survey will be to find out their likes, dislikes, and recommendations for the products they have purchased from you.

The results of a well-crafted and executed Market Survey are like a magic book of success. It has all the secrets: what products your customers want, what they'll pay, what new products or services they wish you had, etc. Information that comes right from your market is the most valuable information you can get your hands on.

Below is an example of such a survey. Be sure to mold this to your business. There are a number of ways to launch this survey, including an online survey, a phone survey, or an in-person interview. Whatever method you choose, do your best to get as many responses as you can. Fifty responses should be the minimum in order to get usable numbers and two-hundred is the desired target.

There are three basic sections to your market survey:

1. Demographics: Make sure you know who is filling out the survey

    a. Age

    b. Income

    c. Zip code

    d. Number of computers in home

    e. Primary spender

    f. Race

    g. Education

    h. Size of business

    i. Years in business

    j. Number of employees

    k. Etc.

2. Market specific questions

3. Request for more info

    a. Open-ended questions

    b. Ask for contact information for possible follow-up (voluntary)

Here are some questions to ask:

1. Which of the following products have you purchased from us?

2. Where did you buy the product?

3. How has the product met your needs since the original purchase? (Extremely Well…Extremely Poorly)

4. Have you ever purchased a product from (competition)? If so, how would you rate that product as compared to the [your product]? (better, same, worse)

5. How often do you use [product]? Weekly, Daily, Monthly, Quarterly, Hourly

6. How easy do you find using [product]? Very, Easy, Neither, Difficult, Very

7. How unique is [product]?

8. How important is the [feature] of the [product]?

9. How likely are you to purchase [product] again in the future?

10. Please let us know what, if any, changes or improvements you would like to see in [product].

11. What additional products would you expect or like to see from our company?

12. How satisfied are you with [product]?

13. How would you rate the quality of [product]? Excellent, Good, Fair, Poor

14. Have you experienced any problems with [product]? Y/N

15. If yes, please describe:

16. Age, education, income, children, marital status, occupation, etc.

Sample Survey

Business Meetings and Networking

1 How often do you conduct business meetings away from your place of business, such as at a coffee shop?

- ○ Daily
- ○ Weekly
- ○ Monthly
- ○ Rarely
- ○ Never

2 If you indicated that you Rarely or Never conduct meetings away from work, please indicate your reason (select all that apply):

- ○ Company has adequate meeting facilities
- ○ Too inconvenient
- ○ Not enough time
- ○ Too far away
- ○ Is not professional
- ○ Need to be near company resources
- ○ Other, Please Specify

3 When conducting business meetings outside of your workplace, where do you meet (select all that apply):

- ○ Coffee shop
- ○ Restaurant
- ○ Gun club
- ○ Adult club
- ○ Library
- ○ Hotel meeting rooms
- ○ Airport business club
- ○ Other, Please Specify

4

When meeting at a coffee shop, which do you frequent the most:

Secondary Research

Find your trade or professional association on the internet (Google Search: [industry] association, or American Association of [industry], or [industry] association of American, or US [industry] association).

On the association's website, look for a link titled Research or Industry. Sift through the links and find any data that is available regarding consumer trends and behaviors. Write down five points of data that are relevant to your business:

1. _____

2. _____

3. _____

4. _____

5. _____

Product Sales

Gather up your sales records, either electronic (QuickBooks) or paper (invoices). Sort through them based on products sold. Look for two trends: the best-selling and the worst-selling product.

1. Best-selling Product:_____

2. Worst-selling Product:_____

Take a look at the two products listed above.

What are the differences between these two products? (color, size, description, price, etc.)

_____

_____

_____

What are the similarities between these two products? (color, size, description, price, etc.)

_____

_____

_____

In your words, why does the first product sell?

Why does the second product not sell?

What changes could you make to your other products to improve their marketability?

THE ONE THING

The One Thing is the product or service that, if available to you, would help you dominate your market. For Dell or Microsoft, it would be a computer that turns on like a light bulb. For a company I used to work for, it was the One Week Final. We were able to complete the installation of a $100,000 audio/video system into a new home so that it was ready to go on move-in day. Sounds like common sense, but in the audio/video industry, it's typical to see the installation company there six months after move-in. What about your industry? Don't let the box get in your way—think outside of it.

Write a description of THE ONE THING that would dominate your market. What does it look like? How does it work? What are the emotional benefits to your customers? Write a single paragraph describing this product:

_____

_____

_____

_____

_____

_____

Maslow's Hierarchy of Needs

Listed in the table below is Maslow's hierarchy of human needs. Finding how your products meet these needs will aid you in developing your Promotion strategy. An honest assessment of how you are promoting your products is important. For example, you may be promoting shampoo as physiological but need to be promoting it as esteem.

For each of your products, list the product(s) that you sell that fit each Need category according to how you are CURRENLTY promoting them. You may not have any products in some categories, and you may have multiple products in a given category. If you have tens or hundreds of products, simply list the product categories, such as shampoos, soaps, detergents, etc.

In the third column, list your products AS THEY SHOULD BE. In other words, if you think a product belongs in an additional or different category, list it there.

Maslow's needs defined:

1. Physiological: hunger, thirst, comfort, body

2. Safety: out of danger

3. Sense of Belonging: affiliation with others, being accepted

4. Esteem: achievement, competence, recognition, approval

5. Understand: knowledge, understanding, exploration

6. Aesthetic: symmetry, order, beauty

Maslow's Need	Current	Adjusted
Physiological		
Safety		

Maslow's Need	Current	Adjusted
Sense of Belonging		
Esteem		
Understanding		
Aesthetic		

Promotion

List three types of promotion that your competition is using. You can be specific. For example, if all three are using the yellow pages, you can list Yellow Pages, Full-page/Half-page, etc.

1. _____

2. _____

3. _____

Are you using any of these methods? If so, are they working?

In the table below, check the boxes next to the methods of promotion that you think would work best for your company and write down the sources in the third column. For example, if you check Advertising, you should list which magazines/newspapers/tv stations you will utilize.

√	Method	Source
	Direct Sales	
	Direct Marketing	
	Advertising	

√	Method	Source
	Public Relations	
	Other	
	Other	

Pain, Solution, Pleasure

What pain does your customer have by NOT using your product? (hunger, lack of transportation, thirst, etc.)

How does your product relieve that pain?

What pleasure is the result of losing that pain? In other words, what are the emotional benefits of using your products?

This Pain, Solution, Pleasure is a great formula for the copy in your promotional efforts, such as the words you use in a direct mail letter or postcard.

Price

In the table below, list the products you would like to focus on. In the first column, list the products that are the core of your business. In the second column, list the prices your competition is charging for similar products. Finally, list your prices in the third column. Realize that your price may be different due to different features or associated services. That's okay. List the actual prices regardless.

Product	Competitors Price	My Price

Product	Competitors Price	My Price

For the products that show a significant difference (>10%), is the price difference causing a loss in sales? Go back and check estimates and bids. Have you lost business because of price?

Your Target Market

Fill in the following (applicable) demographics for each of your major product/ product categories:

Demographic	Product 1	Product 2	Product 3	Product 4
Age				
Family Size				
Marital Status				
Sex				
Income				
Religion				

Demographic	Product 1	Product 2	Product 3	Product 4
Race				
Generation				
Nationality				
Social Class				
Region				
City				

Demographic	Product 1	Product 2	Product 3	Product 4
Occasions				
Other				

CHAPTER 3

▼

SALES

Sales is the process of converting your products into cash. Once your marketing plan has been put into action, it is sales that drives your cash flows. In the marketing section, you defined your market, identified your ideal prospects, and clarified how your products benefit your customers. So, once you have a clear understanding of your marketing plan, making the sale gets much easier.

There are four simple steps to implementing a Sales Plan:

1. Write down your Goals and Objectives

2. Make the "Calls"

3. Conduct the Sale

4. Keep Records

Establish Goals and Objective: And Write them Down!

In making goals and objectives, give yourself very clear and measurable numbers to meet. Your goals will be sales focused. For example, use monthly sales and give it a quantifiable goal to measure. You may also think in terms of new accounts, number of walk-ins, etc. Whatever it is, make sure it is measurable and write it down.

Make the "Calls"

The second step is the most difficult part: making the calls. By "calls," I mean hitting the streets and knocking on doors, making phone calls, or sending opt-in emails. Whatever a "call" means to you, you must do these. This is simply a numbers game. The more calls you make, the more sales you make. The trick is to increase the success rate.

In order to make this easier, there are three things that will help.

1. **Believe in your product.** The more you know and believe in your product, the better you will communicate it to you customer. If you are unsure of your product, that will come across to your customer.

2. **Smile.** There are whole seminars on rapport and body language. To boil it all down to simplicity is to say, "Smile!" It works. Many people don't realize they have a frown built-in to their face. If you need to practice smiling, then practice smiling. An associate of mine even keeps a mirror in her office so that she can put on a smile while doing cold calls. It works, so keep it up!

3. **Enthusiasm.** Again, you must be genuine in your enthusiasm, which comes from believing in your product. When you clearly understand the benefits your customers will get from trading money for your product, you will WANT to make that sale. Bring into your presentation the enthusiasm and joy you feel they are about to receive. Enthusiasm can be conveyed in the personal

sale, a mailing piece, or even a letter. Bring that enthusiasm to your delivery, whether it's a phone call or a drop at the mailbox. Frank Bettger, in his book *How I Raised Myself from Failure to Success in Selling*, says, "I firmly believe enthusiasm is by far the biggest single factor in successful selling."

The 80/20 Rule

Eighty percent of your sales likely come from 20% of your customers. I am sure, if you went back and analyzed your receipts, you would find that 80% of your sales come from a very small group of your customers. There are two things built into this knowledge. First, take care of those 20%. Offer them rewards. Give them discounts or rebates. Make them feel loved. For example, a restaurateur may bring a valued customer from the bottom of the waiting list and get him/her a table as a way of showing his gratitude.

Now take a look at the other 80% of your customers. Typically, they can be divided into three segments:

1. Potential Winners. These are customers who, with some additional attention, could become a part of the top 20%.

2. Nickels and Dimes. These are the customers who don't buy much from you. They may be consistent customers, but they never will become one of your top customers. This segment can be left alone. You don't need to expend valuable energy on these folks. They may be one-time shoppers, visitors, or just stingy.

In either case, this middle of the bottom 80% can be left alone. Treat them well, as always, and they will continue to bring you business.

3. The Trouble-Makers. These are the folks full of complaints, returns, or just take up your time and never buy. You need to get rid of these folks. Adjust your prices for the products they purchase, move them on to a competitor… whatever you need to do, just make sure you move them along because they are using up your most valuable resources: time and money.

Conducting the Sale

The goal here is to help you increase your sales. In other words, if you were to make the same number of calls to the same people you were before doing these exercises, let's make those calls more profitable. Then, when you combine your new marketing efforts and make more calls, you should really see your numbers start to move.

In communicating your sales pitch, I recommend using the Pain-Solution-Pleasure model (mentioned above in the Marketing Exercises). Your clients are feeling some form of pain by not having your products: fear, uncertainty, or discomfort (FUD). Identify that pain and show it to your prospect. Then, offer them the solution to help them feel secure, certain, and comfortable: YOU! You and your products are the solution, so make sure and mention that. Finally, tell a little about the pleasure they will feel by purchasing your products. Your prospect will go through the pain-solution-pleasure with you and realize they need your product.

Strategic Selling

We are talking about making the strategic sale. In other words, we are talking about building relationships with your customers. The stronger the relationship, the more likely they are to come back to you and NOT go to your competition. The three types of selling are Features Selling, Benefits Selling, and Strategic Selling. The differences are in the level of relationship with the customer.

Your first contact with your prospect should be an open discussion in which your customer is doing most of the talking. You can simply repeat some of their statements in the form of a question. For example, if you were selling a home as a realtor and your future homeowner says, "I'd love a split-level floor plan" you could simply respond, "Split level and what else?" This will keep them talking. The more talking a prospect does, the more truth that comes out, the better connection you can make from your products to your customer's needs. This is the process of positioning yourself for the strategic sale.

Let's look at an example, in three different scenarios. The customer is a guy looking for a computer for his home office and enters the computer store:

Features Sale

CUSTOMER: Hello, I'm looking for computer for my home office.

SALES PERSON: Well, I've got a 1.6MHz, Pentium Zelox, hydrogen-cooled, processor, with a dual-whatchamacallit drive....etc., etc., etc. I can give to you today for $3000.

This is a sales pitch pulled off the back of the spec sheet, where the Greek alphabet is listed. Now, if the customer in this case is a techie who cares solely about features, this sales person has made the sale. However, chances are that this customer is more confused than when he walked in.

Benefits Sale

CUSTOMER: Hello, I'm looking for a computer for my home office.

SALES PERSON: The fast processor on this machine will let you get your work done faster. The DVD burner will allow you to store all of your documents electronically, saving you time and space. The high resolution of the screen will allow you to see your documents in much more detail. How much would you pay for that? Well, this one is only $3000.

This sales person has taken the next step in establishing a relationship by pointing out the benefits to his customer. However, he/she has not taken the time to ask questions, and, therefore, is basing these benefits on assumptions. This is a sales pitch pulled off of the front of a spec sheet.

Strategic Sale

CUSTOMER: Hello, I'm looking for a computer for my home office.

SALES PERSON: Last week, you mentioned that your sales folks need to integrate all the information they're bring in from the field. Additionally, you mentioned that you are losing time with large print jobs. So, what I've come up with is a wireless, global networking interface which will integrate your sales force. I also have a print server, which will allow you to share printers while the main one is busy. What you're going to save over the next year is $12000, above the $6000 cost of the computer equipment.

In this case, the sales person has taken time to really understand the needs of his/her customer. The sales person has done research, asked questions, and presented a solution.

Top-Down Sales

Anyone who has been in retail sales has likely learned the craft of Top-Down Sales. Automobile sales people are the best at this. Last time you bought a new car, you were shown to the leather-and-electronics edition of the line. You had to ask to see the lower-priced models (if in fact you did ask). The lesson here is to start at the top. It's easier to work your way down than up. A word of caution here: don't use this as an excuse to stick it to your customers and don't shoot too high. Never take advantage of a customer, as that will have a long-lasting effect on your reputation in the business community. When you qualify your customer, make sure your "top" presentation is within reality. Don't show a Ford customer to a Rolls Royce.

Ask for the Sale

Ask for the sale. Ask for an appointment. Ask for a second meeting. Whatever the objective of your sales call, you must ask for it. The best sales pitch or presentation will fall flat if a sale is not asked for. Many beginners in sales will take a super presentation right up to this point and stop. They assume that customer will start pulling out her wallet and hand over cash. It won't happen that way. Remember our car sales person: "How can I get you into this car today?!" How would you word your request?

This step ties right back into your goals and objectives. How many cold calls did you promise you would make? How much in sales do you need this quarter? The only way to meet these goals and objectives is to make the calls and ask for the business.

The Cold Call

Cold calls are the worst part of sales for most small business owners. If you have a method and a structure, it can be bearable. The key to making successful cold calls is remembering that you are calling an individual person, not some faceless company. There is a living, feeling person on the other end. Think back to when you were cold called. Were you treated like a dollar bill rather than a person? Consider breaking your pitch down into the following four parts:

1. Get Permission. When you finally reach your prospect (getting through the gatekeeper), get their permission to give your pitch. You can flat-out ask for permission, as I do: "I'm calling you cold today to see if there might be an opportunity to do business. With your permission, I'd like to give you my pitch. It's only 60 seconds long, so if you have a minute, I won't take much of your time? Whaddya say?" I either hear a dial tone or, "Sure, go ahead."

2. Make the Pitch. Take them through the Pain-Solution-Pleasure cycle and help them understand the reason they want your products.

3. Ask for the Sale. Again, you must not leave this up to your prospect. You made your case, now ask for the verdict.

4. Consolation Prize. Okay, so you asked for the sale and it was a no-go. Now, you've got somebody who sat through the pitch and said 'no.' Good. They are feeling some guilt. Capitalize on that guilt and ask for a second prize. Get a

referral, an email address for a newsletter, something. Figure out before you start making calls, what consolation prize would help your business.

And remember: Enthusiasm, Smile, and Believe in your Product!

Keep Records

You wrote down your goals and objectives. You also have to write down your sales calls and the results. Keep track of your efforts. For every contact you make, keep track of it: mailings, calls, emails, etc.

The most important aspect of your record keeping is follow-through. If you make a promise (email info, mail literature, etc.), then you must follow-through on that. It's follow-up that will bring you the most loyal customers.

There are many software packages that will help you keep track of your sales efforts:

1. Microsoft Outlook

2. ACT!

3. Microsoft Excel

Whichever you use, make sure to allocate time in your calendar to keep these records up to date. Remember, put this on your calendar, not your to-do list.

Write down at least three sales goals and objectives. Examples of objectives include number of phone calls per week, number of door-to-door visits per week, number of mailers sent per month, etc. Examples of goals include dollar sales per month/quarter and number of units sold per week/month.

The Exercises: Sales

Objectives:

Objective	Per Day/Week/Month
Example: Mailers Sent	500 per month

Goals:

Goal	Per Week/Month/Quarter
Example: Units Sold	1500 per Month

The 80/20 Rule

Go through your list of customers. If you are a retailer, try to come up with different demographic classifications, such as soccer moms, professional moms, family dads, professional dads, single men, single women, trendy teens, etc.

Next, make a list of those customers who represent 80% of your sales. This list will likely turn out to be roughly 20% of your customers. If it doesn't, then go back and take a look and see if you can re-classify your list or find some other reason.

Study the list of your 20% performers. Get to know them.

Write down a plan for how you are going to make sure you keep these top customers. How are you going to show them your appreciation? Write that plan here:

_____

_____

_____

_____

_____

_____

Now take a look at the bottom 80%, those who are not the top customers. If you can, divide them into three groups using the process of elimination. First, identify the diamonds in the rough. In other words, separate out those customers who, with a little additional attention could become a top customer for you. Then, identify those customers who cost you money (these are the customers with unreasonable returns, complaints, or just take up too much of your time).

Devise a plan for how you are going to make those diamonds in the rough shine. Are you going to launch a specific marketing campaign just for them? Are you going to call them? Send them letters? Offer coupons or other incentives? Write your plan here:

_____

_____

_____

_____

Identify a plan for how you are going to fire your trouble customers. Consider using a statement similar to: "I don't think we can help you meet your [specific] needs; you might consider using [competitor]." Or, try: "I'm afraid we're not the right company for you; we can't meet your expectations; why don't you give [competitor] a try." Write your plan here:

_____

_____

_____

_____

Now for the most important part of the 80/20 rule plans: DO IT! You've got three good plans here; now go put them into action. Put the plan on your calendar right now!

Top-Down Sales

The goal of this exercise is to help you increase your sales by simply changing your offering. There are three parts to this exercise.

First, get out your bids/estimates/invoices for the last 6–12 months. Take a good look through them. Find the times when you offered a lower-end product when you realistically COULD HAVE offered a higher-end one. For example, look for times when you could have sold the $65 shirt when you actually showed and sold the $55 shirt.

Write down a sampling of the times you undersold your customer:

_____

_____

_____

_____

Now, look at the bids/estimates/proposal/prices that you are currently offering your clients. The key here is to find future sales opportunities to sell the best first or, at least, to OFFER the best first.

Based on the above list of missed opportunities, write down the opportunities before you to conduct Top-Down sales:

_____

_____

_____

_____

A note of caution: don't go nuts unless you KNOW you can go nuts. In the example above, we went from a $55 shirt to a $65. We didn't go from a $55 shirt to a $400 shirt. Keep this realistic, but find real opportunities to offer the best and increase your sales.

Ask for the Sale

As we mentioned, the car salesman's famous line is, "What do I need to do to put you in this car today?" As much as we hate hearing that question, we can feel it working on us. What question can you ask your prospects to get them to sign up? Write it here:

_____

_____

Keep Records

Buy or develop a system for keeping track of your sales efforts. At a minimum, you must keep the following information on each prospect or lead:

1. Name

2. Contact info: phone, email, fax, address, etc.

3. Date of initial contact

4. Date of each follow-up contact

5. Notes which correspond to follow-up dates

6. Flags which let you know a follow-up is required

CHAPTER 4

▼

LEADERSHIP

Leadership is the glue that binds all other parts of your business, namely your Focus, Marketing, Sales, and Finances. Leadership is easier than most people think. Contrary to popular belief, charisma is not required. The simple, key principles of leadership can be implemented by anybody, including you. Leadership can be learned. Being born with leadership skills is not required.

There are four basic steps to establishing yourself as a leader:

1. Develop a Targeted Vision

2. Communicate the Targeted Vision

3. Give and Receive Feedback

4. Give People What They Need to Succeed

Develop a Targeted Vision

It is important to develop a vision that targets those you are leading. Your targeted vision is different from your company vision, but it must support the company mission and vision. The targeted vision should be customer-oriented. What benefit do your products bring to your customers? The targeted vision should help the crews, teams, and people understand this benefit to the customer. Is it a matter of speed, professionalism, customer service?

The second element to the Targeted Vision is inspiration. The key here is to be inspirational. The Targeted Vision should ring loud like a slogan or a title of a fight song. All those who are being led should be able to repeat this Targeted Vision with energy in their voice. This slogan should play a key role in helping employees stay motivated to come to work and make their contributions to the company's cause.

As an example, in my last company, we installed high-end audio-video gear into luxury residential homes. Typically, in this business and its industry, the final installation begins when the homeowner moves into his/her new home and lasts one to six months. Knowing that this is a very stressful time for the new homeowner, we decided it would be better to be FINISHED on their move-in date. At first, this idea was met with laughter. However, we turned it into a Targeted Vision: The One-Week Final. In other words, we would complete the job in one week and be finished on move-in day. Laughter turned to pride when we achieved this goal. That achievement would not have been possible without the Targeted Vision.

This Targeted Vision helps your team understand the Why of what they do. They begin to want to contribute. They feel excited to come to work. Morale is high and goals start getting checked-off.

Communicate the Targeted Vision

The next step in the leadership process is communicating the Targeted Vision. Can you imagine, developing this Targeted Vision, letting everybody know what it is, then never mentioning it again? Then, six months later when the time comes to finally hit the finish line, you pronounce to all, "Okay everybody! Remember six months ago when we established our Vision? Well, it's now time..." Of course that would seem ridiculous. This Targeted Vision must be communicated to the team over and over and over. Put it on their checklists, inside their vehicles, in the restrooms, on the bulleting board, anywhere they will see it. Even if the crews meet this with laughter, keep it going.

The final element of communicating the Targeted Vision is to make your expectations very clear. Let them know the performance measures, the attitudes, and the feedback from them that is expected. By simply stating, "We expect you to let us know what you need to make this vision a success." Let them know what you expect.

Feedback

Feedback is to be received and given. In communicating the Targeted Vision, it is important to listen to your team members and to provide them proper feedback on their performance. The frame of reference in both cases is in letting them know your expectations. A simple statement of, "We expect..." will lay the ground work from which feedback can be used to make necessary adjustments.

When I was in the military, I was a platoon leader of a PATRIOT Missile platoon. Our Targeted Vision was to "Be the Go-To Platoon." That was our mantra. It wasn't, "We're going to be the most proficient, highest-trained platoon in the battalion with the highest physical fitness tests…" No, we're simply saying, "We're the Go-To Platoon!" That was clear and kept the whole team on the same sheet of music. The point here is letting the team know what is expected of them.

We expected them to become certified on their equipment. We expected them to contribute as individuals to the team effort.

Make sure your employees know they can come to you and give you feedback. Make sure they know that their ideas will be heard. Something you can try with them is to ask them to leave a legacy. I learned from a fellow officer in the Army to leave a legacy at every place you work. Offer your employees the same. Ask them to leave a legacy in their positions. They will come to you with ideas, suggestions, and recommendations. Listen to them and make those gems into legacies.

In letting your team members know your expectations, it becomes easier to steer them in the right direction. If an employee is slacking off, letting the others down, it can be as easy as saying, "We expect everybody to contribute to our efforts. We are about to achieve great things, and I'm sure you want to be a part of that, right? I'm sure you'd prefer to make a contribution."

Feedback also plays a key role in helping your team members get themselves motivated to contribute. People are self-motivated. Everybody on your team wants to contribute. Your job is to provide an atmosphere of feedback that enables them to get motivated.

People motivate themselves by acquiring a number of forms of positive feedback, namely money, recognition, promotions, job titles, etc. It is your job to figure out what each member of your team wants. Some will want to be recognized with certificates and awards. Some will want to be assigned the special projects. All will want the most cost-effective method of recognition: a Thank You.

If you can figure out what your team members use to get themselves motivated for work, you will be able to get the most out of them. They will go the extra mile for you, *willingly*, even without asking.

A simple Thank You goes a thousand miles and cost you nothing. It is important to recognize the efforts and skills of your employees. It is very likely that you hired these folks to do work that you either do not want to do or don't have the skill to do. In either case, make sure you let them know how much you appreciate their skill and hard work. It goes so far to simply say, "Wow, Steve, I really admire your ability to work with our customers! I wish I had that patience." Steve will be one happy camper and will likely have a bounce in his step that may last for days. And that was free.

Give Your People What They Need to Succeed

The biggest mistake you can make in establishing yourself as a leader is to do the first three steps, then saddle your people by NOT giving them what they need to create the vision. It's no help to tell them, "Now go do great things, but you have to get all purchases signed by me!" You must give them room to succeed. This sounds like common sense, but what happens is business owners see it more like giving them room to fail. Yes! You must give them room to make mistakes. With each mistake, they take more responsibility and take more ownership in your cause.

It can be difficult as a business owner to give employees the freedom to act on their own judgment. Doing so will show them you have confidence in them and will empower them to act in behalf of the company. Take the famous example of the Ritz-Carlton. Their employees, all of them, are empowered to spend up to $2000 a day to take care of Ritz customers. Can you imagine? That is trust and team building. You need to display a similar trust in your people. Give them what they need to turn your vision into reality.

Ask your people daily, "Do you have everything you need to be successful today?" There are two sides to this question. First of all, you are showing them that you are committed to the vision and to their part in reaching that vision. Secondly, you are holding them responsible for their part in things. If they need something they don't have, it's their responsibility to make sure they get it. By asking the question, you are making them aware of that responsibility.

Put Together a Winning Team

As you start thinking about leadership, it is vital that you put together a winning team. Whenever I hear a company complain about their people (turnover, can't find good help, etc.) I start looking at the leadership. It is easy to keep a bad employee. It is also very harmful to do so. One of the reasons employees leave a company is that they see the owners keep a lousy employee—a person with a bad attitude, a poor work ethic, or just plain sloppy. This sends a bad message, loud and clear: we have no standards.

There are three parts to building a winning team. First, get rid of the bad apples. An employee with a poor work ethic or a negative attitude is like a virus in your business. He/she will have a negative effect on the whole organization. Get rid of these viruses immediately. Now, be sure to follow your states employment laws and consult an attorney if you need to. You don't want to get yourself in trouble. However, the most important thing here is to get rid of the rotten apple. You will notice an immediate effect on your team. Their morale will improve immediately and work will get done faster and better.

The second part of building a winning team is hiring the right talent. This can be hard for small businesses. If you find somebody out there who you know would help your business, go get 'em. It's okay to steal employees from other companies. The point here is if you need a power forward, go get one.

The final piece of the team puzzle is getting people into the right jobs. If you see a good person struggling, the reason may be the job he or she has been assigned. Find out where the passion is for that person and get them in the right seat.

The analogy for the process is the Bus, by Jim Collins, author of *Good to Great*. The key is to get the right folks on the bus, the wrong ones off, and make sure the rest are in the right seats.

The Exercises: Leadership

A Focused Vision for those You Lead

This Vision can be looked at as a team slogan. It must be inspirational, obvious, and brief. It must pertain to your team's daily tasks, but point to a final goal. This concept should be a grand vision, one that could change the industry.

Here are some examples:

Industry	Vision	Associated Goals
Automotive	Putting Safety on the Road	Keep a clean shop Conduct safety checks Communicate to customers Educate customers
Retail Store	Send 'em home happy	Assist shoppers Show them the options Ask for the sale Smile
Professional Service	Sharing wisdom	Educate clients Ask questions Be there for them

The process to establishing a team vision:

Pull it from the company vision. Which part of the company vision rests in the hands of your team?

What is the action that your employees take? In other words, what Verb are they doing? Is it selling, closing, maintaining, installing, relating? Write down a single verb or action that describes your teams daily purpose:_____

_____

What is the Object of that action? In other words, what is the material result of your employees actions? Is it a contract, a cash receipt, an installation, a customer, a good, a service? Write it here:_____

_____

What emotional benefit do your customers get from this action/object creation? What need is your team helping to satisfy by taking these actions? Is it comfort, health, well-being, security, convenience, sense of belonging, self esteem, entertainment, order, understanding? Why are they buying this product? Write it here:_____

_____

The final step here is to add inspiration. If you could get your team to perform its work faster, better, or different from your competition in such a way that it would be a strong competitive advantage, what would that be? Would it be speed, quality, or difference? Another way to think about it is: what is the one complaint about your industry? Is it honesty, time-to-complete, availability of products? What is it? Complete this sentence: If we could just _____, we would clean up our competition!

Takeyouranswerstotheabovethreequestionsandmakeasentencehere,intheform of: Our team [verb] [object] [differentiator] in order to help our customers [benefit].

_____

For example: Our team repairs computers overnight in order to help our customers stay in the game!

Next, rephrase that sentence in a shorter, more inspirational form. Usually, an easy way to do this is to eliminate "Our team" and change the verb to an active verb ending in 'ing.' For example, Keeping your business in the game! This forces the timeline and clearly adds to the company's vision. Write your ideas here:

_____

_____

_____

_____

Finally, circle the one idea that feels best. Put it on a piece of paper in large letters so you can see it. Look at it for a few days and imagine communicating this to your team. Make necessary changes. When you know you've got it, communicate it!

Communicating the Targeted Vision

Post your Targeted Vision in the following places, if appropriate. Remember, this vision is for your team, not for your customers.

1. On memos or other documents that go to team members

2. Bulletin boards

3. Inside vehicles

4. In clipboards

5. On the door (in employee areas)

6. On cubicle walls

7. In the break room

Feedback

Remember that people are motivated by the following:

1. Recognition: "Thank You", Awards, Certificates

2. Money: Bonus, Raise

3. Promotion: Titles, Authority, Responsibility, Management

4. Prestige: Vehicle, Title, Uniform, Training/Certifications

For each of your team members, indicate which of the above is self-motivating to each. Then, indicate one or more actions you can take at the appropriate times to assist them with their self-motivation.

Team Member	Motivated By	Actions to Take

Team Member	Motivated By	Actions to Take

Provide the Resources they Need

In your next meeting, ask your team members the following questions. You may wish to ask these on a one-on-one basis, but a group will often provide better results.

1. What can we do to make your job easier?

2. If you were the CEO/President of this company, what changes would you make to help the team be successful?

3. What changes are you afraid we'll make?

4. What tools are you missing that would help you be successful?

Now, asking the questions is great, but it's worthless without action. Take notes, discuss the issues, and MAKE CHANGES. The most important phase of leadership is giving your team the opportunity to be successful. They will work very hard to make your company a success as long as there is a sense of purpose and they are given freedom to create and perform.

Fill Up your Bus

You already know who needs to get off the bus. Take the following actions. Consult a Human Resources expert in your state to find the procedures to terminate an employee. In general, you must give them a poor review, wait for results, and then make the firing. In either case, start the process TODAY. This process helps the employee get on with his/her life and it sends a clear message to your employees.

CHAPTER 5

▼

FINANCIALS

I ask all of my clients to sign an agreement before working with me. In this agreement, they sign to the fact that the purpose of their business is to be profitable. What does it mean to be profitable? Well, we can take a book definition:

Profit is what remains after all costs have been subtracted from a firm's total revenue.

Therefore, to be profitable means to have revenues that exceed expenses, right? Almost. To remain in business, you must do two things. First, you must be able to buy goods from your vendors. With nothing to sell, what's there to sell, right? Second, you must be able to pay your employees. When you reach a point that you cannot buy goods and you cannot employ help, then you are out of business. Therefore, to be profitable means that you have the cash you need to keep your doors open by paying vendors and employees.

So, how do you make sure that you remain profitable? You must understand one very simple concept:

Cash is cash. Everything else is accounting.

Don't get caught up in your financials to the point you lose site of your cash balance. What all of the accounting methods, software packages, and high-priced accountants add up to is one simple concept: cash is king. You must have enough cash in the bank account to pay for the business.

Cash Conversion Cycle

For a business that buys and sells on credit, understanding how to convert a sale into cash is vital. There is a fancy accounting term called the Cash Conversion Cycle. This fancy phrase boils down to this: get paid faster than you pay your vendors. It is vital to your cash balance that you collect payment from your customers before you pay your vendors. Don't take this to mean that you should withhold payment to vendors until you get the check in the mailbox, but in your collections process you should be thinking this way.

There are a few practical ways to sway the Cash Conversion Cycle in your favor:

1. Start accepting alternative payments: credit cards, debit cards, PayPal, etc.

2. Negotiate with your vendors to get extended terms (turn COD into net-30).

3. Change your contracts/payment structure to receive more payments that coincide better with predicted payments to vendors.

Cost of Trade Credit

Do you get invoices from your vendors with terms that read: 2%10 net 30, or similar? If so, you are staring at a very important decision on your part. What this term means is: "pay me at 10 days or at 30 days and not at any other day." Let's take a look at this.

If you see the discounted net terms on an invoice, what it means is that your vendor has essentially decided to finance you at a rate of 2% over twenty days. This annual percentage rate turns out to be 36.7%! What a favor! Let's say you buy an item for $100 and you get the bill with 2%10 net 30. This means the actual cost of the item is $98. If you choose to wait and pay the bill from days 11 to 30, you are paying 2% in financing for the benefit of your vendor letting you keep their money for those extra days. So, if you buy a large quantity of goods and are constantly paying vendors, you have a lot to lose by letting your vendors finance you, namely 36.7% APR interest. Can you afford that?

The conclusion on the net-terms is to pay your invoice at day 10 or day 30. If you are going to pay the financing charge, you might as well have the cash in your account for the full thirty days.

The Financial Statements

If cash is the lifeblood of your company, then the financial statements are the x-ray machine, the stethoscope, and the blood pressure meter. There are three financial statements that will tell you your company's past, present, and future: the income statement, the balance sheet, and the cash budget, respectively. Understanding these statements, even in the slightest bit, will help ensure the success of your company.

The Past: The Income Statement

The income statement is the famous P&L statement, profits and losses. It is very basic, in that it takes the sum of revenues and expenses over a given time period and lines them up to see. The top of the income statement is the Revenues, Cost of Goods Sold, and resulting Gross Profit. Following that are your expenses. At the bottom, or THE BOTTOM LINE, is the net profit. This net profit is what feeds cash into your business.

The most important thing to know about the Income Statement is what the numbers represent. If you are on an Accrual basis, that means the numbers represent "booked" business. In other words, you sign a deal, it gets booked as revenue right away. This is NOT cash! If you are on an accrual basis, make sure you understand this, and do not let yourself be misled. I have seen companies with millions in profits (accrued) go out of business due to the lack of cash.

If you are not on accrual basis, then you are on a cash basis (much easier to read). This means that when a check arrives, it is booked as revenue. In this case, the Income Statement will be a good snap-shot of your true profits. In either case, the Income Statement is telling you how your company performed in the past. Were you profitable?

Finally, the income statement holds the final judgments as to how you spent your money. By taking some of the expense items (marketing, advertising, training, etc.) as a percent of revenue, you can measure their effectiveness. We'll look at this in the exercises below.

The Present: The Balance Sheet

The Balance Sheet is a record of your assets, your liabilities and your equity taken as a snapshot of the current situation. A Balance Sheet tells you how much cash, accounts receivable, accounts payable, loan balances, etc. that you own right now. What the balance sheet tells you is how liquid and solvent you are. In other words, if you needed money from the bank or special credit from a vendor, how likely are they to extend you the credit? The goal is to have more assets than liabilities. Reading and understanding the balance sheet will help you get there.

The Future: The Cash Budget

The Cash Budget is basically a projected Income Statement. Take a look at a good history of Income Statements. Depending on how long you've been in business, you may have 36 months of statements or just a few. In either case, use your Income Statements and try to project out into the future what you think your sales, cost of goods sold, and expenses will be for the next three years.

The Exercises: Financials

Cash Conversion Cycle

First, here are some definitions:

• Sale: Getting your customer to commit to purchasing your product.

• Purchase Order: Placing an order with your vendor for goods sold

• Inventory: Items from vendor have arrived and been processed

• Invoice Out: You have sent an invoice to your customer for payment

• Pay Invoice: You have sent the payment to your vendor

• Cash: You have received payment from your customer

Vendors	P.O.	Inventory	Pay Invoice (-)	
YourCo	Make the Sale		Invoice Out	Cash (+)

How long is it between receiving the vendor invoice and paying the invoice: _____ days

How long is it between sending out your invoice and receiving payment: _____ days

How long is it between receiving your customer's payment and making the payment to your vendor: _____ days. Which comes first, your cash or payment to vendor:

_____

Based on your answers above, how could you adjust your billing procedures to make sure you have more cash on hand?

_____

_____

_____

It is possible that your company keeps a constant inventory, making it nearly impossible to tie your purchases to your sales. In this case, you should take a look at how fast your inventory turns over. See Appendix A: Inventory Turnover and the Cash Conversion Cycle.

Building the Financial Statements

Building the Financial Statements is not fun. It's also not as hard or scary as it may seem. The thing we're trying to get to here is to get you another perspective on your business. You are simply gathering some real data, in the form of sales receipts, invoices, bank statements, credit card records, etc. If you have one bank account for the whole of your business, then the statements alone may provide you all the information you need.

You can do this and you must do this! When I ask successful entrepreneurs how often they check their financials, they all respond in kind: constantly!

Building the Income Statement

AT A MINIMUM, you should put together three income statements:

1. This month-to-date

2. Last month

3. Last 12 months

You should seriously consider doing the last year in quarters.

You will need the following records:

1. Revenues

   a. If you are cash basis, use deposit slips

   b. If you are accrual basis, use invoices

   c. In either case, do your best to figure out how much money you have brought in over the chosen time period (month, quarter, year)

2. Cost of Goods Sold

   a. Invoices paid from vendors

   b. Receipts from vendors

3. Other Costs

   a. Materials receipts

   b. Parts receipts

4. Expenses

    a. Gather all receipts for the categories listed on the income statement below

    b. Any receipts you have for legitimate business expenses that don't fit a category (these will be included in the General and Administrative or the Miscellaneous lines).

Keep these around for the Balance Sheet exercise, too.

Now, fill in the Income Statement. If you have Microsoft Excel, you can download this form from http://www.mybusiness-advisors.com/seminars/forms. Or, you can download it directly from Microsoft's website.

Building the Cash Budget

Remember, the Cash Budget is a projection into the future. In this exercise, you will make two significant changes to the Income Statement:

1. Take the same format and project it out twelve months (at first)

2. Add the cash equation to the bottom: Beginning of Month (BOM), End of Month (EOM), Cash from Operations.

Instructions for filling out the Cash Budget:

1. Sales: Take the values from your Total Sales in the income statement. You may need to make adjustments to account for the season and for growth. Project out your sales.

2. Collections: Do your best to figure out how you collect your CASH. If you are signing contracts, do you take deposit, progress and final payments? If you are a point-of-sale retail business, do you offer credit?

3. Disbursements

   a. Salaries: This is the actual cash out in the month. In other words, this is the checks you write to you and your employees.

   b. Payroll Expenses: Take a percentage of payroll, anywhere from 15% to 25%

   c. The rest of the entries mimic the Income Statement. Be sure to use historical data and project out.

   d. As you go through this, try to think of annual payments that will pop up

      i. Vehicle registrations

ii. Membership dues

iii. Insurance premiums

4. Cash, BOM is taken from the Cash, EOM after Borrow in the previous month.

5. Cash Receipts is the Total Cash Receipts line in the Collections section

6. Cash Disbursements is the Total Cash Disbursements line

7. Cash from Operations: subtract Disbursements from Collections

8. Cash, EOM: add Cash from Operations to Cash, BOM

9. If your Cash, EOM is negative, you will need to borrow. In that case, enter here the amount you need to borrow. Keep in mind: you may want to keep a MINIMUM cash balance at all times, just in case. Account for that additional cash when determining how much to borrow.

10. Cash, EOM after Borrow is Cash, EOM plus the borrowed amount. AS LONG AS THIS LINE CAN BE KEPT IN THE POSITIVE, YOU ARE STILL IN BUSINESS.

Now, fill in the Cash Budget. If you have Microsoft Excel, you can download this form from http://www.mybusiness-advisors.com/seminars/forms. Or, you can download it directly from Microsoft's website.

Building the Balance Sheet

Much like you did for the Income Statement, you will need some of your records. See the list in the Building the Income Statement section.

Remember, the Balance Sheet is a snapshot of your situation RIGHT NOW. So, as you sit right now, fill in the blanks for the balance sheet:

1. Current assets are assets that you could convert into cash within six months to a year.

2. Long-term investments are stocks and bonds of other companies, expected to be held for over a year

3. Property, Plant, and Equipment includes furniture, building, land, machinery and other items with a long useful life. These items will depreciate over a given period of time. Consult your accountant for these values. If you don't have an accountant, use a five-year life with depreciation being 20%, 32%, 19$, 12%, 11%, and 6% over years one through five, respectively. Take the percentage of the Property, Plant and Equipment for each item. This will give you a good guess.

4. Current Liabilities are payable within one year, e.g. short-term loan.

5. Long-term Liabilities are payable after one year, e.g. SBA loan.

6. Retained earnings SHOULD equal your net income plus your beginning equity

7. If this is your first go around, this will not balance. It balances if Total Liability and Shareholder's Equity is equal to Total Assets.

Now, fill in the Balance Sheet. If you have Microsoft Excel, you can download this form from http://www.mybusiness-advisors.com/seminars/forms. Or, you can download it directly from Microsoft's website.

Key Ratios and Metrics

Now that you've built the financial statements, let's take a look into them and discover some things about your business. Listed below are a few common metrics, or ratios, that are used to analyze a business:

Working Capital = Current Assets-Current Liabilities. This is the amount of cash you have to run your business.

Current Ratio = Current Assets divided by Current Liabilities. This should be a value greater than one (1). Make it a goal to raise this value to about 1.5.

Debt to Total Assets = Total Liabilities divided by Total Assets. This, like the current ratio, should be greater than one (1). This ratio will determine how likely you are to get additional credit for your business. Make it a goal to get it above one.

Profit Margin = Net Income divided by Total Sales. Does this measure up to your industry?

In addition to the ratios listed above, you should consider having your own, internal ratios. We call these 'metrics' and they can be vital to your success.

Here are a few examples of metrics other companies use (*Good to Great*, p. 106–107):

• Profit per Employee, Abbott Laboratories

• Profit per Customer, Gillette

• Profit per Customer Visit, Walgreen's

You might consider some others:

1. Profit Margin

2. Sales per month

3. Advertising as a percent of sales

4. Marketing as a percent of sales

Write down two metrics that, if you kept a constant eye on them, would help you guide your business to success:

1. _____

2. _____

CHAPTER 6

▼

PUTTING IT ALL TOGETHER

Now that you've completed the exercises, the most important step is to integrate these concepts and ideas into your business. My concern is that you will take this completed workbook and set it aside, hoping to use some of the ideas in your daily grind. What I would like you to do is use your work here as a system within which to run your business. You see, the concepts here in this book are not a list of separate concepts. They are all interconnected and make up a working system. For example, your Mission Statement is connected to your Sustainable Competitive Advantage, your Marketing Plan, your Sales System, and your Leadership concepts. Understanding the needs that your products help fulfill is connected not only to your Marketing Plan, but is also a key part of generating the enthusiasm needed to believe in your product and make the sale.

If there are any exercises that you skipped or partially completed, take some time to go back and finish those up. I have made it a point to include only useful exercises and each one has a particular, distinct lesson. So, now is the time to get them all done and get your workbook complete.

What you've got here is a working business plan, so make sure you work it. Read it at least once a month (make this a recurring event on your calendar). Make changes to it as you go. The point is to make sure that you maintain a big picture view. Some of the exercises were designed to help you do this:

1. Post your mission statement

2. Make the dashboard a part of a meeting

3. Post you dashboard and update it frequently

If you do these things, you will do yourself a lot of good in keeping that bird's eye view of your business, your market, and your competition.

The final note here is on Passion. The one concept that truly touches all others directly is your Passion. When you went through the exercises and conjured up that old Passion for your business, you really felt that Passion work its way through you. You need to find a method to bring up that passion at will. You will need it when things are not-so-good. You will need it just before making those cold calls. You will need it when you meet with customers. You will need it when negotiating with vendors. Therefore, you need to find a way to bring that Passion to a boil. Find a piece of music that helps. The truth is, you were just able to bring the Passion to the surface. Figure out how you did that. You've already got a tool to use in this matter.

That's it. You've done it. Congratulations! I think you have taken an important step in becoming the successful entrepreneur you always knew you would be. Find the strength, the resolve, to determine that you will not fail, that you can only succeed. As Abraham Lincoln said, "You cannot fail if your resolutely determine that you will not fail." You can only succeed if you resolutely determine that you will succeed.

Oh, one last thing. If you are not a member of your local chamber of commerce or a local networking group, then get out there and get involved. The meetings are fun, and you will meet good business contacts. Don't expect immediate business. It will take time to get referrals as people get to know you. Your time at these functions is well spent and will set you apart from your competitors. So, go sit down at Google, get out the business section of the local papers, and find some groups to get involved with.

Good luck, my friend and Good Business!

Please send me an email at spreston@mybusiness-advisors.com and let me know your thoughts on this book, your business, or what the weather is like in your area.

Thanks for trusting me and taking the time to read my book. I hope it was helpful.

Appendix A

▼

Inventory Turnover and the Cash Conversion Cycle

1. Pick a time period. The best one is annual, but you can pick a half-year, a quarter, or even a month. How many days are in this time period: _____ (year: 365; semiannual: 180; quarter: 90, month: 30).

2. Average Inventory: What is the average inventory, in dollars, that you maintained over this period? You can add beginning inventory and ending inventory and divide by 2: _____ dollars.

3. Total Cost of Goods Sold (COGS): What is the total Cost of Goods Sold during that period? _____. If you don't know this answer, finish the Financials section first. Look at the Income Statement, which should provide the answer here.

4. Divide Total Cost of Goods Sold (#3) by the Average Inventory (#2): _____ _____. This is the number of times you turn over your inventory in your time period.

5. Divide the number of days in your time period (#1) by the number of times you turn over your inventory (#4): _____. This is the number of days you turn your inventory over.

6. The value in #5 should, typically, be between 30 and 45 days. Anything lower, and you may be losing opportunities due to empty shelves. Anything over that, and you may be tying up funds in inventory. Remember: Inventory is frozen cash.

Notes:

Notes:

978-0-595-38027-5
0-595-38027-1

www.ingramcontent.com/pod-product-compliance
Lightning Source LLC
Chambersburg PA
CBHW030840180526
45163CB00004B/1401